That Fat Cat

That Fat Cat

Poems for Youngsters

Eric Leif Davin

DavinBooks
Box 90087
Pittsburgh, PA 15224

That Fat Cat
Poems for Youngsters

For Youngsters of All Ages

Animal Crackers

That Fat Cat

That fat cat
    Walked in on little fog feet,
    Not looking at all for a treat to eat.
And there on the mat he sat,
    Replete with meat
        And proud of his feat.
    That fat cat
        Is oh, so neat.
He opened his jaws,
    Licked his paws,
        And did not pause
            For any laws
            Or your applause.
But that fat cat
    Will let you pat
        His fluffy fur
    Or, should you prefer,
        Scratch beneath his chin,
            To see him grin.
        Then, with a purr,
That fat cat
    Curled up in the heat,
        Tucked in his feet,
And that fat cat
    Took a nap
        On the mat.

Amanda Panda Bear

Lying in her lair,
Just like any Panda Bear,
Amanda Panda had no care.
It was a lazy hazy day
And there simply was no way
Anyone would dare
To stare
Or muss a single hair
Of Amanda Panda Bear.

And just beneath her lair
There was a crooked stair
Which randa
To the sanda
Where Amanda Panda
Kept her pairs of pears
And other wares,
Like her flute of jute,
Her bamboo shoots,
Her business suits,
And worn out boots.

And there, amid the scattered loot,
She'd sit and toot
Upon her flute
Until the sun was high.

And then she'd sigh,
And wave bye-bye
And climb back to her lair,
Where, upon the air, if I do not err,
One could hear the roar
(Or was that snore?)
Of Amanda Panda Bear.

Raccoona Raccoon

Quick!
There in the dark,
The dogs bark
As she runs through the park.
There!
In the light of the moon,
Blink too soon
And you'll have missed
Raccoona Raccoon,
Gone in the mist!

She knows when you doze,
And despite all your measures,
She uses her nose to expose
All your hidden treasures.
Her quick paw
Is not a claw
With which to gnaw.
It's like your hand.
And when the night grows cold,
She uses it to pan
In the sand
For hidden gold.

You've got to hand it
To this furry bandit.
In a flash
She'll make hash
Of your trash.
Before you turn around,
It's on the ground,
And away she'll bound,
Never to be found.

In her Lone Ranger mask,
She's fast at her task.
On the lookout for danger,
She's the seldom seen
Bandit Queen.

The dark wind blows
And her little toes
Are almost froze,
But away she'll race,
And is gone
With no trace!

The Butterfly Forest

Summer snowflakes,
A flitting colored chorus
Of flying flowers,
Sipping nectar by the hours.

The sun awakes
Nature's florist,
Who heeds the call
And gives to all
The Butterfly Forest.

The Viceroy trails
The Monarch and his Queen
Around whom quickly teem
The Tiger Swallowtails.

There the Polydamas
And the misnamed Polyphemus
Both are on the fly.

And there, against the sky we spy
Two friends of mine,
Spicebush and the old Buckeye,
Along with Hackberry and Pipevine.

And here is dainty Painted Lady
With her lovely White Peacock.
All will surely speak
Of her Great Purple Hairstreak.

And you should hear the talk
Of how she did provoke
The Mourning Cloak
As he awoke
And then was heard to mutter
He was the very poorest
Of all of those who flutter
In the Butterfly Forest.

Birds of a Feather

Packed tight,
Like beads on a string,
Birds perched on the wire.
More lit,
And the birds,
Jostling, flapping, complaining,
Bumped down the wire.

And then they were gone,
A flickering cloud,
Fading away.

Bluejay Day

High in the sky,
The bluejay
Has the day
In which to play.
He never pays,
Or so they say,
To fly and lay
In the warm sun rays.
He takes his time
In the bright sunshine,
And then,
At end of day,
He flits away.

Grackles in the Grass

Are those crows
Cackling on the lawn
At the crack of dawn?
Oh, heaven's no,
Those black birds
Aren't crows,
As any bird watcher knows.

But, since you ask,
Those are grackles in the grass.
See how they step
Through the new pearl dew
On big yellow feet?
Only grackles are so neat.

And only the grackle
Will cackle
So shrill
Through such a yellow bill.

And no matter what the weather
His shiny feather
Shimmers from afar
Like oil on a road
Of bright black tar.

So, heaven's no,
        Those aren't crows
                Or raving ravens,
Laughing on the lawn
        And cackling in the grass
                At the crack of dawn.
But, since you ask,
        Those noisy nosy fellows are
                Grackles in the grass.

The Owl Takes Flight

When the night dogs growl,
And the wolf does howl,
That is when this fowl
Is on the prowl.
It is in the cowl
Of the night
That the owl
Takes flight.
Sitting like a star
Way up high
In the sky,
His huge great eyes
Gather in the night light
And he spies
From afar
The sight
Of skittering feet.
The owl takes flight
And falls from his height
Like a silent kite.
He grips his prey
And then is gone,
Away in the night.

Penguin in the Wind

The penguin, they say,
Is a flightless bird,
In a word,
A bird
That cannot fly
In any way,
Though it might try
The live-long day.
But who are "they" who say
The penguin cannot fly
In any way,
Though it might try?
Have they felt the wind
That blows
Across the snows?
Do they know
How it spins and sends
Everything high
Up in the sky?
And when it flows
Across the snows,
The penguin knows
To catch the wind,
Which then will send
Him flying high
Up in the sky.

“They” say the penguin
Cannot fly,
But I have seen a penguin
High up in the sky,
Flying in the wind.

Night Flight

Out of the night,
With the fading light,
Comes the dark flight
Of the bats!

Their sight is poor,
And yet they pour
From their cave exactly right.
They know where they are,
They have their own radar!

These bats are not a nasty blight,
They are the farmers' friend,
For there really is no end
To their appetite
For bugs and grubs
And crawling slugs
And pesty flying gnats.

They twist and bend
Upon the evening wind
And then they drop
Along the top
Of the sleeping farmer's field
To help him with his yield.

They mop
Up every bug in sight
That crawls or flies or hops
Among the farmer's crops.
That farmer really should adopt
This furry friend
Who comes to lend
His help 'most every night.

And as the East turns bright
With the coming of the sun,
His hungry work is done,
And so, it seems,
Is his night flight.

The Ant

The tall mushroom stands
Stark white in the short damp grass,
Ignoring the ant.

Frantically the ant
Crosses the mottled middle
To the crimped edge.

It hesitates there,
Then races through the middle
To the other side.

Back and forth it runs,
Edge to edge, and back again.
Then – Over the edge!

Boris the Thesaurus

Boris is such a nerd
He knows all the words
You ever heard,
And then ten thousand more!

Thick as a brick,
But quick as a lick,
He tells you all you need to know
About this and that,
Any old word
Only he has heard.
The short, the long, the wild, the trite,
Those out of sight,
And many more!
What a dinosaur!
Turn to Boris when you need a word.
He'll give you one
You never heard.
Or one that means the same,
But lacks the fame,
And with a twist.
He just can't resist.
That's Boris the thesaurus!

People Poems

Astro Flu

What do astronauts do
When they get the flu?
How do they blow their noses?
Use hoses?
Do they have a messy view
After they ker-*choo!*
And spray the faceplate
With icky goo?
Wouldn't you just hate
To share their fate?
Eeeeeeuuuuuuu!
What a zoo!
I don't know what I'd do.
Hold that sneeze till I was blue.
Wouldn't you?
What *would* you do
If you, too,
Knew
You had the flu?
Would you sit and stew?
And say, "Oh, *poo!*"
Would you boo-hoo?
(Better watch that tear!)
I know what I'd do:
Stay right here
With a tissue near
And the least of my woes
Would be blowing my nose!

The
Defective Detective

Down on the floor,
        I was taking a nap
                After placing a tap
On the lines of my very own phone.
Then there came a loud rap
        At my office door
And I deduced I wasn't alone.

In came this dame,
        It was always the same.
She sneered at my stubble,
        And I could tell she was trouble
                With a capital "T,"
        And that rhymes with "P,"
And that stands for "Pay me!"
        She said, as I crawled into bed.
She was my mean landlady
        And I'd already spent
                This month's rent.
"You're three months late
                And I can't wait.
“I'm mighty selective
        About my tenants,
                And so I sentence
                        You to blow, Joe.

You haven't been effective
Since you were a defective
on this city's police farce.
Your cases are sparse
And you got no dough,
So out you go!"
Yeah, she was trouble,
With a capital "T,"
And that rhymes with "P,"
And that stands for
"Poor, poor, pitiful me!"

Maya's First Ride

The square was bare that summer night,
Nothing there but pale moonlight.
But with the dawning of the day,
A gay array was on display.
A fair was there, from just nowhere,
With slides and rides
And more besides:
A carosel had come to dwell
Beside a deep dark wishing well,
Which rang a bell and gave a yell
And your fortune it did foretell.

But of the many sights and sounds
Of which this carnaval did boast,
It wasn't jugglers or the clowns
That little Maya liked the most.
It was the wheel, the Ferris wheel,
Which held the utmost of appeal.
It made her reel,
It made her squeal,
And she could not quite conceal
The way it really made her feel.

She had to ride, she did decide,
Forget about the rest.
No matter where you may reside,
You can search the countryside,
You can hire an expert guide
To take you 'round the whole world wide,
And all will surely fail the test,
The Ferris wheel's the very best.

Maya stepped up to the line
And paid the man her only dime
To ride the wheel -- her first time!

Having paid the man her fare,
And feeling very debonaire,
Maya sat down in the chair,
Like a TV millionaire
Having won a dreadful dare.
He strapped her in and with a spin,
Sent her way up in the air.
Upward, skyward, went the chair,
And as the wind blew back her hair,
Maya lost her every care.

Upward, skyward, went her flight,
And, despite the awesome height,
Maya found to her delight,
She had not any bit of fright.

Northward, southward, went the ride,
        Up above the countryside.
Higher, faster, further, farther,
        Up above the far hillside.
And a crowd began to gather
        Calling others come outside!
Come see Maya on her ride!
        Forward, backward, up and down,
High above the old playground.

High above the boulevard,
        High above the old church yard,
High above old Scotland Yard!
Higher than the birds and bees,
        Higher than the highest trees,
Maya looked down on all the people,
Looked down on the tall church steeple,
        Looked down on the circus clown,
And in a voice that did resound,
        She yelled out to the ground,
"I am never coming down!"

That did astound
        Those gathered round,
Standing spellbound on the ground,
Staring at the girl up there,
        Swinging way up in the air.
And though they begged her
        Most profound,
Through the day into the night.
        Maya laughed in her delight,
        And she would not come on down.

"We need a ladder to get at her,"
Someone said, getting madder.
"Why not use a helicopter?"
"Better yet, a flying saucer!"
And the teacher and the preacher
And the super and the trooper
All began to jabber
Of the many ways to grab her.

Then they built a winding stair,
And climbed it way up in the air,
To Maya rocking in her chair.
But when they got up in mid-air,
Maya simply wasn't there,
Maya wasn't anywhere!

So, child, when you also do decide,
To take your first wild circus ride,
Have a care, do beware!
Don't stay all the way up there
Swinging high up in the air.
Come on down, to the ground,
Or we won't find you anywhere!

Le Belle Rachelle

Awake! Awake!
          Don't forget the date!
Don't be tardy,
          Don't be late!
                    Get in line!
                              Come and dine,
          It's party hardy time!

Don't say nay!
          Ride the sleigh!
Come in any way you may!
          Today's the day,
                    The day we say,
Happy clappy birthday!

We'll fill the hall from wall to wall!
          Le Belle Rachelle
                    Is the belle of the ball.
Her nights have teemed
          With ice cream dreams,
And now's the day she has it all!

Is she six?
You want some kicks?
Is she seven?
Oh, my heaven!
Wait! She can't be eight?
If you want some cake,
Do not mistake,
Rachelle is nine!
And that's so fine!
It's party hardy time!

Awake! Awake!
Don't be late!
And bring a gift,
Or she'll be miffed!

Brave Rachelle, She Did Not Yell

Brave Rachelle, she did not yell
When she fell
And broke her arm.
She turned so pale,
But did not wail,
Did not quail,
Did not rail
About such harm.
She looked at it and simply said,
"Oh, dear, oh dear, oh, dear, oh darn!"

And then she asked
All of her friends,
From the first unto the last,
To come to her
And write upon her cast.
They came so fast,
From hill and dale,
And mountain vale,
From up and down and all around,
That she was aghast!

They rang the bell,
They used the mail,
They used the telephone to tell.
Some set sail against the gale,
And some were let out of the jail.
Until the lookouts on the mast
Cried out, "Avast!
Here come lots more from the past!"

And then at last the vast
And mighty horde
Had finished with its task.
And brave Rachelle was never bored
With reading all the names of friends
Who came to make her well
By writing on her cast.

Mollie's Dollies

There once was a girl named Moll,
Who wanted more
Than just one doll.
She'd go to the mall
And buy them all,
The long, the short, and the tall.

She had dolls that were fat
And dolls that were thin,
Dolls made of muslin,
Dolls made of tin,
And painted dolls of Greek porcelain.

She had foreign dolls from over the seas,
And a baby doll that always pees.
And a very large batch
Of adopted dolls
From the Cabbage Patch.
But, you see, there was a catch,
None of them would ever match!

She had dolls that were tattered,
And dolls that clattered,
She even had dolls
That always chattered,
Not that it mattered.

She'd come back from the marts,
Hauling them home
In full grocery carts,
There were dolls with missing hearts,
And various body parts.
And as she patched up a knee,
Mollie said, "Gee,
Can't everyone see,
My dollies need me!"

She must've had at least a million,
But she wanted an even billion,
Or maybe even a trillion,
Or maybe even a big gazillion,
All to put in her dollie pavilion.

Oogie Boogie

You should see
Oogie do the Boogie,
The latest dance from France.
You'd slap your knee
And laugh with glee,
To see my Oogie prance.
Oh! You'd have no chance!
His very stance
Would put you in a trance!

Oh, that Oogie, what a clown!
The faces that he makes,
The vases that he breaks,
All the stories that he fakes!
There's never any tear or frown
When my Oogie is around!

And he's always in the stew
Doing things he shouldn't do.
He always slams the outer door,
Tracks the mud across the floor,
All these things and much, much more!

Anything that's broken,
Any naughty word that's spoken,
The answer's still the same,
It's Oogie who's to blame!

But he is my closest friend,
And you should see his silly grin!
But, no matter how you stare,
You won't see him by the stair.
He isn't there!
Or anywhere!
He's invisible, you know,
Which makes him quite invincible
Wherever he may go!

So, no matter how you try,
No matter how you cry,
You won’t see Oogie do the Boogie,
The latest dance from France!

Traces of Braces

There are flowers on the faces
Of little girls with braces:
Two lips.
And 'twixt them,
Are the traces of braces.

They shine and gleam,
And truly seem,
The very highest fashion.
Better than cases
Of shoe store laces,
A day at the races,
Or ancient Chinese vases.

They form the very basis
Of a little girl's smile
As she dips and clips,
For hours and hours,
All the flowers
Around the bowers;
The peppermint,
the doublemint,
Mint julips and the camomile.

And then she snips
The smallest tips
Of rose petals and rose hips,
And slips them in the cup
From which she sips
And smiles.
And there, between the lips,
Traces of braces,
On little girls' faces.

Chores Are Bores

Chores are bores,
    As all the children know
        Deep down to their cores.
We all abhor
    To mop the floor
        And polish up the door.
We all ignore
    Our parents' roars
        To do our daily chores.

But wait! Before it's way too late!
    What if no one
        In the whole wide world
    Ever did a chore?

What if you tore
    The clothes you wore
And no one sewed them up?
    It'd be so sad to look so bad,
        And what is more,
    You'd look so awful poor!
And do you think he'd feel so glad
    If no one fed the pup?
And what about your cluttered room
    If it never saw a broom?

Could you lay your sleepy head
Upon your only bed
If all your toys and other junk
Covered up your bunk
And fell across the floor?
Up to the roof the mess would soar
And then into the hall would pour
When you opened up the door.
What a yucky sight!
You know it simply isn't right
To put up such a fight.

Chores are bores, but here's the way
To turn them all into play:
A teensy, weensy, little bit,
Done each and every day,
Will tame the biggest baddest bore
And make it go away.

The Green-Eyed Monster

You just can't wait!
        You've got a date
With your best playmate
                And you can't be late!
There she stands by the school yard gate,
        Waiting there just for you.
But then you see there's someone new!
        She's not alone, there are two!
She's laughing with another girl,
        And it sends you all awhirl!
Oh, my goodness! What a sight!
        Shall you run, shall you fight?
She's your one and only friend,
        And you really can't pretend
                That it really doesn't send
        You quite around the bend!
And then the Green-Eyed Monster
        Whispers in your ear
                Just the thing you fear,
        That you've really lost her.
But, now, don't you be a fool,
                Don't you lose your head,
        He's a mean and nasty mobster
                Who'd rather see you dead.

Try to play it cool,
Don't listen to that ghoul!
Dump that Monster in the dumpster!
'Cause, now, don't you see,
There's no need for jealousy!
You still rate
With your playmate,
As she hugs you close as close can be,
And says, "Instead of you and me,
Now the two of us are three!"

Your Grandmother

One way or the other,
You'll need your grandmother.
You can call her grandmom,
Or even grandma,
But never grandpaw!

When you're late, she'll wait,
She's always there,
You know she'll care.
Her pantry's never bare,
And she'll always bake
The very best cake!
You love that homey kitchen smell,
And you can always tell
When she's cooking up a spell
Of magic cookies, oh, so well!

She reads you stories from her books,
As she tucks your covers tight,
And looks in all the nooks,
For scary creatures of the night.

And when your mother is away,
Mom-mom is sure to stay.
And when you want to play,
Grandmom will find a way.

And though she may be short and stout,
        Like a teapot with a spout,
You will never see her pout,
        You will only hear her shout,
When she sees you come about.

She hugs you close with open arms,
        Keeps you safe from all the harms,
So I need not go much further --
        You know you need
                your old grandmother!

Gabby the Great:
A Tale of Ancient Splendor

Gabby the Great
Rises above all.
Below this great and mighty head
Ten thousand slaves sweat
To finish before sunfall.

Gabby the Great
Will view the work at dusk.
The colossal bust must
Be finished,
Lest Gabby the Great be displeased.

Gabby the Great:
A behemoth of stone
Towering a mile above the desert.
A monument built
With blood and bone.

Gabby the Great
    Stares toward the horizen.
    The scream of a falling slave
    Breaks the monotony of
    Cracking whips
        And bellowed curses.
    The work goes on.

Gabby the Great:
    Ten thousand slaves labored
    For seventeen years
        To complete this
    Monolithic statue.
    The last stone is fitted into place.
    The work ceases.

Gabby the Great
    Is finished.
    For the first time
        In seventeen years
    The slaves, their drivers,
        Their overseers, and
    The planners rest.

Gabby the Great
    Looks upon herself
        And smiles.
    She strides to her chariot and,
    With a last look back
    Gives this command:

"Gabby the Great
Is pleased with your work.
It is a noble and
Magnificent monument
To myself.
However –
it is in the wrong place.
It catches my mood better
Over there.
Move it."

Gabby the Great
Motions to her driver
And is gone over the sands.

Books

I have a warm feeling for my books,
And for the adventures they extend.
I open their pages with an eager mind,
To me, they are my friends.

I've sailed the seas and roamed the jungle,
Climbed the Alps & searched for treasure.
Fought in wars and seen great men,
Their bravery beyond measure.

I've rescued damsels and fought the ogres,
Feared the dragons, as did knights of old.
I've lived a life of rich and poor,
And into slavery I've been sold.

I've lived a life of full content.
The sights I saw, the trips I took,
They're so easy to acquire --
Just read a book.

Eric Leif Davin
8th Grade, Age 12

www.ingramcontent.com/pod-product-compliance
Ingram Content Group UK Ltd.
Pitfield, Milton Keynes, MK11 3LW, UK
UKHW040028200726
13854UKWH00001B/409

9 781387 191499